Architectural Luxury. Theories of architecture and issues facing the field today

Armstrong Odiwuor

Bibliographic information published by the German National Library:

The German National Library lists this publication in the National Bibliography; detailed bibliographic data are available on the Internet at http://dnb.dnb.de.

ISBN: 9783389026489
This book is also available as an ebook.

© GRIN Publishing GmbH
Trappentreustraße 1
80339 München

Print and binding: Books on Demand GmbH, Norderstedt, Germany
Printed on acid-free paper from responsible sources.

The present work has been carefully prepared. Nevertheless, authors and publishers do not incur liability for the correctness of information, notes, links and advice as well as any printing errors.

GRIN web shop: https://www.grin.com/document/1452833

Architectural Luxury: Theories of architecture and issues facing the field today

By

Armstrong Odiwuor Okanga

Table of Contents

Introduction

Architecture has served as a representation of society, reflecting the successes, values, and even the fall of civilizations throughout history. According to Andersen (2018), it is the science and art of designing buildings.[1] As a practice, architecture ranges from the total built environment at the macro-level to furniture and product design at the micro level. Therefore, the theory of architecture became the acknowledged translation of the term *ratiocinatio* as utilised by the first century Roman engineer-architect, Vitruvius, to distinguish between practical and intellectual knowledge in architectural education. However, according to Chestnova (2022), this now signify the foundation for evaluating building projects and buildings' merit.[2] These sound judgments or assessments are a crucial aspect of essential aspect of the whole creative process of architecture. Elsemary (2015), for instance, argued that buildings can be designed by a continuous creative, intellectual dialectic between reason and imagination in the creator's mind.[3] In this context, theories are very important to luxury architecture because they establish the foundation in which architecture depends on, or supposed to be. Therefore, this paper will analyze fourth architectural theories that relate to Architectural Luxury, key issues for architecture today and the effects of architectural sites. Finally, it will discuss the architectural changes and their effects on society.

---

[1] A. U. Andersen, "Translation in the architectural phenomenology of Christian norberg-schulz," *Architectural Research Quarterly* 22, no. 1 (2018)

[2] E. Chestnova, *Material theories: Locating artefacts and people in Gottfried semper's writings* (Taylor & Francis, 2022),

[3] Y. Elsemary, "Architectural Theories and Design Methodologies Investigating the nature of relation," 2015, xx, Arab Academy for Science, Technology & Maritime Transport.

Architectural theories

The Phenomenon of Place by Christian Norberg Schulz

The theory of phenomenon of place, as developed by Schulz, emphasized converting the environment into meaning by the invention of new places. According to Andersen (2018), Schulz's theory insisted on both the spirit of the place as well as its sensuous qualities, which may include symbolism, colors, lighting and materials.[4] In essence, it provides that basic architectural component such as the ceiling, floor or wall are important and experienced as frame for nature, boundary and horizon. However, Lindstrom and Malpas (2020) considers the Phenomenon of Place a descriptive theory since it attempts to distinguish between space and place, and also prescriptive because it identifies the light on the phenomenology.[5] This phenomenology became a very influential school of thought for modern architects like Peter Waldman, Tadao Ando, leading to a revived interest in the sensuous qualities of color, light and materials, as well as in the tactile, symbolic importance of the joint.

Consequently, Holcombe (2015) argued that a place's structure should be described with regards "settlement" and "landscape" and assessed through categories "character" and "space."[6] According to Mehaffy (2020), "space" symbolizes the three-dimensional organization of the place elements, while "character" symbolizes the overall "atmosphere."[7] Rather than differentiating between character and space, Schwartz (2016) points out that it is possible to use

[4] A. U. Andersen, "Translation in the architectural phenomenology of Christian norberg-schulz," *Architectural Research Quarterly* 22, no. 1 (2018):
[5] R. Lindstrom and J. Malpas, "The modesty of architecture," *Political Theory and Architecture*, 2020
[6] L. Holcombe, "*The architecture of Luxury*, by Annette Condello," *Luxury* 2, no. 1 (2015)
[7] M. W. Mehaffy, "The impacts of symmetry in architecture and urbanism: Toward a new research agenda," *Buildings* 10, no. 12 (2020)

a comprehensive concept like lived space.[8] In this context, similar spatial organisations can have relatively differing characters based on the concrete treatments of all the elements that define space. While the history of the basic spatial forms.

Universal Space theory

According to Tiesdell and Carmona (2015), this theory begins with the opposite assumption that aspects of the space use change with time.[9] Therefore, an undifferentiated space where several activities can be carried out with minimal adjustments is required. Chestnova (2022) argues that instead of analysing the atoms, the Universal Space theory devises a whole.[10] In this context, architects try to develop a house which does not attach a particular site or client to the project(s). For luxury proposes, the note of individuality of a house depends upon the particular site, and it is flexible enough to serve one family's ever-changing needs and the different needs of various families.[11]

Consequently, the freedom for experimentation allows other unique elements, for instance, great openness both to the interior and exterior.[12] This has increased the demand for these kinds of spaces that are not highly adaptable or responsive to various uses at different times but also qualifying based on the needs of different users. According to Mihai (2020), the entire phenomenon leads to the establishment of the Universal Space.[13] Furthermore, scholars like Andersen (2018) consider this theory descriptive because it identifies the type of space that is

---

[8] C. Schwartz, *Introducing architectural tectonics: Exploring the intersection of design and construction* (Taylor & Francis, 2016)

[9] S. Tiesdell and M. Carmona, *Urban design reader* (Routledge, 2015),

[10] E. Chestnova, *Material theories: Locating artefacts and people in Gottfried semper's writings* (Taylor & Francis, 2022),

[11] N. Lahiji, *An architecture manifesto: Critical reason and theories of a failed practice* (Routledge, 2019)

[12] I. F. Pane et al., "The study of the influence of functionalism and international style on architecture development in Medan city," *IOP Conference Series: Materials Science and Engineering* 309 (2018):

[13] M. Mihai, "The architecture of political renewal," *Political Theory and Architecture*, 2020,

enough to house different uses that range from sports and leisure to industrial activities.[14] For instance, a big single-volume enclosure is a space that is flexible and can be adapted or modelled to fit the need of nearly every user.

Functionalism

Functionalism or 'form follows function' is a theory which proposes that the main purpose of a building(s) should be the beginning of its design instead of its aesthetics. According to Pane et al. (2018), it is linked to the early-20th century modernist architects, and it suggests that, instead of a building being designed according to stylistic trends or past precedents, its purpose would dictate its form.[15] According to Kaschina and Nesterova (2018), functionalism has become a foundation for modernist architects, for instance, Frank Lloyd Wright argued that function and form are one, rendering decorative aspects as superfluous.[16] However, functionalism is criticised for its overt focus on form rather than functionality and practicality.

Furthermore, according to Kaschina and Nesterova (2018), the idea that a building is defective until the space provided is appropriate and adequate for their desired usage seems apparent.[17] However, this is controversial due to different reasons. First, while there are no exact statistical ways to compute spatial appropriateness or adequacy, there are several elements or types of building for which a person cannot confidently establish the optimum dimensions and forms. Secondly, buildings are often used for reasons besides the original plans. Similarly, doubt exist on whether "function follows form" or "form follows function" since in general, it can be

[14] A. U. Andersen, "Translation in the architectural phenomenology of Christian norberg-schulz," *Architectural Research Quarterly* 22, no. 1 (2018):
[15] I. F. Pane et al., "The study of the influence of functionalism and international style on architecture development in Medan city," *IOP Conference Series: Materials Science and Engineering* 309 (2018):
[16] I. V. Kaschina and A. N. Nesterova, "The problem of affirmatively architectural form and structural functionalism," *Materials Science Forum* 931 (2018)
[17] ibid,.

assumed that the task of an architect is to building particular spaces to fulfil the predetermined functions. According to Mihai (2020), evidence suggests that most key social institutions have originated from already built-up spaces.[18] A good example is the evolution of parliamentary systems such as the British system, which was founded upon the idea of a legislature in which the opposition and government confront one another. According to Pane et al. (2018), the systems originated from the fact that the earliest parliamentarian met in the medieval palace chapel.[i] The seating was designed according to the liturgical specifications of a Christian church.

Theory of Signs

Geoffrey Broadbent provided a guide to the theory of signs by offering a considered discussion of the semiotics of architecture and presented a proposal for architects deliberately designing meaning into their structures.[19] Historians like J.M. Richards, Nikolaus Pevsner and Giedion, and architects like Charles Jencks, Brent Brolin, Charles Moore, Mies, Walter Gropuis and Le Corbusier, had forcibly argued that luxury architecture should not be about just styling that is cosmetically applied to the buildings' exterior.[20] Instead, according to his theory, a building symbolises or at the very basic "carries" meaning. Referencing Even Pevsner, Broadbent argued that every building or structure creates a link in the beholder's mind, whether desired by the architect(s) or not.

However, according to Audring and Masini (2019), Broadbent presented his perspective towards meaning, as well as how to derive benefits from his theory.[21] For instance, he argues that

---

[18] . Mihai, "The architecture of political renewal," *Political Theory and Architecture*, 2020

[19] J. Audring and F. Masini, *The Oxford handbook of morphological theory* (Oxford University Press, 2019),

[20] E. Chestnova, *Material theories: Locating artefacts and people in Gottfried semper's writings* (Taylor & Francis, 2022)

[21] ibidn, Audring and Masini

a building is going to symbolise something, irrespective of the worst or best intentions of the architects. In this context, Dadfar and Heydari (2018) believe that an understanding of the way buildings symbolise can help architects develop and design them to do it effectively.[22] Consequently, while introducing Peirce and Saussure's theory, Broadbent developed a general signification theory, to show the way one thing, anything, for instance, a building, smoke, rain clouds, diagram, picture or a word, reminds of or stands for a theory called Semiology or Semiotic.

According to Dadfar and Heydari (2018), semiotic is divided into three levels, syntactic, semantic and pragmatic.[23] First, the syntactic deals with a blend of signs, for instance, how words are joined or merged to form sentences irrespective of their specific meanings or significations or their link to the behavior(s) in which they happen. Secondly, the pragmatic deals with the origins of the uses by the architects as well as the impacts of signs on the individuals interpreting them within a variety of behaviors in which they happen.[24] Lastly, the semantic concerns the signification of signs in all signifying modes, with how they really "carry" meaning(s).

Key issues for architecture today

One of the greatest challenges facing contemporary architecture is the need to create and preserve the heritage. According to Andersen (2018), large-scale urbanisation has led to a race to use steel, iron, concrete and glass to construct the biggest, tallest and the most magnificent

---

[22] S. Dadfar and F. F. Heydari, "The impact of urban parks on citizens' place attachment (Case study: Bagh Mohtasham of Rasht)," *Asian Journal of Water, Environment and Pollution* 15, no. 2 (2018):
[23] ibid,. Dadfar and Heydari
[24] ibidn,

buildings.[25] Consequently, in order to match up, architects started to use similar methods and a consequence of which the cultural fabric of urban societies disintegrated. According to Elsemary (2015), cities across the world look alike when it comes to materials and style of buildings.[26] Therefore, architects have had to utilise their knowledge of the past and visions for a better future to reinvent the lost character of cultural cities before the need to assimilate replaces their unique identity. Consequently, while architects are not entirely independent, they have a specific responsibility to their clients. Therefore, conflicts with peers and colleagues, political powers and the pressures of globalisation and modernisation can often overwhelm them.

Secondly, architrave is also facing the challenge of material limitations. According to Lindstrom and Malpas (2020), architects do not just design beautiful buildings, they have to complying with changing building codes and accommodate customer buying patterns in the market.[27] However, finding the precise or right material is often a difficult endeavor for contemporary architects who sometimes can or cannot accept the right information concerning technical product specifications. Specifically, getting a manufacturer to understand the need to aggressively proceed with digitising product specs and increase delivery speeds.[28] Therefore, architects must be able to effectively specify the required materials.

Design for inclusivity is the third major challenge facing architecture. This results from the fact that people now live longer, and ethnic, economic and gender boundaries are now fading as the internet is progressively globalising the world.[29] Therefore, architecture is now looked

[25] A. U. Andersen, "Translation in the architectural phenomenology of Christian norberg-schulz," *Architectural Research Quarterly* 22, no. 1 (2018):

[26] Y. Elsemary, "Architectural Theories and Design Methodologies Investigating the nature of relation," 2015,

[27] . R. Lindstrom and J. Malpas, "The modesty of architecture," *Political Theory and Architecture*, 2020,

[28] I. F. Pane et al., "The study of the influence of functionalism and international style on architecture development in Medan city," *IOP Conference Series: Materials Science and Engineering* 309 (2018)

[29] J. Audring and F. Masini, *The Oxford handbook of morphological theory* (Oxford University Press, 2019)

upon not only to design and create luxurious structures but also environments that are both inclusive and sensitive and generate awareness among the users to each other's needs. According to Holcombe (2015), this is considered instrumental in nurturing open-mindedness as well as an acceptance of humanity and its multifaceted personas.[30] In this context, architecture must be mindful of such factors and develop inclusive and considerate measures for both the wellbeing and comfort of the various strata.

The effect(s) of the architectural site

According to Tiesdell and Carmona (2015), architecture exists to establish a physical environment people live in.[31] However, it is more than the built environment, it is part of human culture, and represents the way people view themselves, and the world. Consequently, architectural sites not only affect society on the highest level, it does so on a personal level, profoundly impacting its occupants. From the layout to the luxurious material finishes, architectural site contributes towards people's productivity, mood and health. For instance, according to Schwartz (2016), people who work or live in well-designed and luxury spaces are more focused, less likely to be sick and contribute more to the society.[32] on the other hand, unimaginative, concrete and sterile buildings and landscapes cause high stress levels. To combat this, architects design buildings and cities that are beautiful, luxurious, and creating mindful connection to nature.

Secondly, well-designed architectural site as well as the connection people have to it cannot be easily quantified. Yet, according to Mihai (2020), the feeling of walking spaces that

---

[30] L. Holcombe, "*The architecture of Luxury*, by Annette Condello," *Luxury* 2, no. 1 (2015)
[31] S. Tiesdell and M. Carmona, *Urban design reader* (Routledge, 2015),
[32] C. Schwartz, *Introducing architectural tectonics: Exploring the intersection of design and construction* (Taylor & Francis, 2016)

feel right, is both functional and resonates with individuals on subconscious levels.[33] Luxury architectural sites are designed bearing in mind that while designing for function is very important, it is also crucial to tap into emotional connection because they all contribute the sense of experiencing architecture. According to Kaschina and Nesterova (2018), this is not merely an intellectual understanding but also a connection between the site and user themselves in an emotional manner.[34]

Lastly, according to Swope (2021), for the outcome to have a unique impact on the occupants' environment and the building's efficiency, the architect must address elements including, site location, local climatic characteristics, arrangement of spaces, building envelope, and building orientation and geometry.[35] Architectural sites that combine their physical surroundings with the use of the principles of green design effectively often provide greater physiological and psychological benefits for the society.[36] An architectural site must be positioned relative to the environment, and is adjusted to the natural resources like wind and solar energy, which increases quality of pace and energy efficiency.

Changes and how they have improved society

In the field of architecture, the term luxury is now being viewed in a positive light. According to Dadfar and Heydari (2018), by emphasising state-of-the-art technology and attention to detail, architects provide users with unique solutions.[37] Therefore, testing the notion

[33] M. Mihai, "The architecture of political renewal," *Political Theory and Architecture*, 2020,
[34] I. V. Kaschina and A. N. Nesterova, "The problem of affirmatively architectural form and structural functionalism," *Materials Science Forum* 931 (2018):
[35] Curtis Swope, "Is Green the New Red? Marxism, Ecology, and Contemporary Architectural Theory," *Humanities* 10, no. 1 (2021)
[36] I. F. Pane et al., "The study of the influence of functionalism and international style on architecture development in Medan city," *IOP Conference Series: Materials Science and Engineering* 309 (2018)
[37] S. Dadfar and F. F. Heydari, "The impact of urban parks on citizens' place attachment (Case study: Bagh Mohtasham of Rasht)," *Asian Journal of Water, Environment and Pollution* 15, no. 2 (2018):

of 'luxury equals expensive,' today the focus is on building something awe-inspiring and rousing. While architecture was based solely on fulfilling the needs of societal and was more functional rather than ornamental, it involved conventional construction and designs techniques fused with remnants from a Corbusier-inspired aesthetic.[38] Many people frowned upon exposed interiors and 'luxury'. However, according to Elsemary (2015), the view of luxury has shifted significantly and is now being viewed through a positive lens.[39]

According to Andersen (2018), the abandonment of the conservative opinion on architecture has left a more evolved view on deluxe interiors and luxury buildings.[40] Consequently, with the rise and spread of affluence, this has led to a higher acceptance and appreciation of grandeur. In essence, society has become progressively inclined towards enjoyable lifestyles, and the market for high-end, innovative décor and spaces is increasing. According to Pane et al. (2018), what was considered inaccessible is now essential and therefore, the luxury has continued to take its place commonplace lifestyle as opposed to an intermittent indulgence.[41]

Similarly, the urge to reinvent and evolve our surroundings has been met by consistently trying to improve on earlier practices. According to Dadfar and Heydari (2018), luxury not appropriately fits into this societal desire for a better life, thus, fulfilling the need for competence, comfort, and the aspiration to dream.[42] Holcombe (2015) argue that luxury is not

---

[38] Y. Elsemary, "Architectural Theories and Design Methodologies Investigating the nature of relation," 2015,
[39] ibid,.
[40] A. U. Andersen, "Translation in the architectural phenomenology of Christian norberg-schulz," *Architectural Research Quarterly* 22, no. 1 (2018):
[41] I. F. Pane et al., "The study of the influence of functionalism and international style on architecture development in Medan city," *IOP Conference Series: Materials Science and Engineering* 309 (2018)
[42] S. Dadfar and F. F. Heydari, "The impact of urban parks on citizens' place attachment (Case study: Bagh Mohtasham of Rasht)," *Asian Journal of Water, Environment and Pollution* 15, no. 2 (2018)

extra-ordinary but a natural progression of a changing economy, of which the entire society is playing a contributing role.[43]

Lastly, with the increasing population pressure and the expansion of urban boundaries into satellite towns, there has been a need to redevelop infrastructure to address the societal demands.[44] For instance, safe and efficient public transport, better civic amenities, hygienic and safe waste disposal tactics, as well as an emphasis on providing multi-functional spaces for the general public are the key issue architects are incorporating in the cities' redevelopment plans.[45]

Conclusion

Architectural luxury includes interiors and exteriors that that strive for an unburdened, minimally programmed spaciousness in which meaningful and simple moments can freely unfold. Over the years, luxury architecture has been progressively celebrated and it is not a privilege of the elite or leisure class any more. Instead, it has become ubiquitous and practically anyone can experience it. Therefore, focusing on various contexts, this paper has discussed four key theories of architecture that relate to luxury, including The Phenomenon of Place, Universal space theory, functionalism and the theory of signs. In this context, there are issues for architecture including the need to design for inclusivity, material limitations, and preserve the heritage. Consequently, architectural site contributes towards the society's productivity, mood and health. Finally, this paper has shown that in the field of architecture, the term luxury is now

---

[43] L. Holcombe, "*The architecture of Luxury*, by Annette Condello," *Luxury* 2, no. 1 (2015)

[44] I. V. Kaschina and A. N. Nesterova, "The problem of affirmatively architectural form and structural functionalism," *Materials Science Forum* 931 (2018):

[45] Curtis Swope, "Is Green the New Red? Marxism, Ecology, and Contemporary Architectural Theory," *Humanities* 10, no. 1 (2021):

being viewed in a positive light, unlike before when it was frowned upon. This has led the

society to accept and appreciate luxury architecture more.

Bibliography

Andersen, A. U. "Translation in the architectural phenomenology of Christian norberg-schulz." *Architectural Research Quarterly* 22, no. 1 (2018), 81-90. doi:10.1017/s1359135518000088.

Audring, J., and F. Masini. *The Oxford handbook of morphological theory*. Oxford University Press, 2019.

Chestnova, E. *Material theories: Locating artefacts and people in Gottfried semper's writings*. Taylor & Francis, 2022.

Dadfar, S., and F. F. Heydari. "The impact of urban parks on citizens' place attachment (Case study: Bagh Mohtasham of Rasht)." *Asian Journal of Water, Environment and Pollution* 15, no. 2 (2018), 37-46. doi:10.3233/ajw-180016.

Elsemary, Y. "Architectural Theories and Design Methodologies Investigating the nature of relation." 2015. Arab Academy for Science, Technology & Maritime Transport.

Holcombe, L. "*The architecture of Luxury*, by Annette Condello." *Luxury* 2, no. 1 (2015), 109-112. doi:10.1080/20511817.2015.11428568.

Kaschina, I. V., and A. N. Nesterova. "The problem of affirmatively architectural form and structural functionalism." *Materials Science Forum* 931 (2018), 817-821. doi:10.4028/www.scientific.net/msf.931.817.

Lahiji, N. *An architecture manifesto: Critical reason and theories of a failed practice*. Routledge, 2019.

Lindstrom, R., and J. Malpas. "The modesty of architecture." *Political Theory and Architecture*, 2020. doi:10.5040/9781350103771.ch-014.

Mehaffy, M. W. "The impacts of symmetry in architecture and urbanism: Toward a new research agenda." *Buildings* 10, no. 12 (2020), 249. doi:10.3390/buildings10120249.

Mihai, M. "The architecture of political renewal." *Political Theory and Architecture*, 2020. doi:10.5040/9781350103771.ch-013.

Pane, I. F., M. N. Loebis, I. Azhari, N. Ginting, and D. D. Harisdani. "The study of the influence of functionalism and international style on architecture development in Medan city." *IOP Conference Series: Materials Science and Engineering* 309 (2018), 012021. doi:10.1088/1757-899x/309/1/012021.

Schwartz, C. *Introducing architectural tectonics: Exploring the intersection of design and construction.* Taylor & Francis, 2016.

Swope, Curtis. "Is Green the New Red? Marxism, Ecology, and Contemporary Architectural Theory." *Humanities* 10, no. 1 (2021), 45. doi:10.3390/h10010045.

Tiesdell, S., and M. Carmona. *Urban design reader.* Routledge, 2015.

ⁱ ibid, Pane et al.

14